Earning, Saving, Spending

Banks

Margaret Hall

Heinemann Library
Chicago, Illinois

Designed by Depke Design
Printed in China

08 07 06
10 9 8 7

Library of Congress Cataloging-in-Publication Data
Hall, Margaret, 1947-
    Banks / Margaret Hall.
        p. cm. - (Earning, saving, spending)
    Includes bibliographical references and index.
    Summary: Introduces the purpose and functioning of banks, including information on checking accounts, ATMs, debit cards, and reading a bank statement.
    ISBN 1-57572-231-3 (lib. bdg.)   ISBN 1-58810-337-4
    1. Banks and banking-Juvenile literature. [1. Banks and banking.] I. Title.
HG1609.H35 2000
332.1-dc21   99-047428

Acknowledgments
The author and publishers are grateful to the following for permission to reproduce copyright material:

Cover photograph: PhotoEdit/Dana White, (top), Photodisc (bottom).
PhotoEdit/Davis Barber, p. 24–25; PhotoEdit/Michelle Bridwell, p. 14; Mike Brosilow, pp. 26, 28-29; PhotoEdit/Tony Freeman, pp. 7; 11; PhotoEdit/Spencer Grant, p. 6; PhotoEdit/Jeff Greenberg, p. 15; The Picture Cube, Inc./Eunice Harris, p. 22; Ben Klaffke, p. 5 (left); PhotoEdit/Phil McCarten, p. 4; PhotoEdit/Michael Newman, pp. 5 (right), 16; Photodisc, pp. 8, 10, 12, 18, 19, 20, 21, 23, 27; Dana White, p. 17; PhotoEdit/David Young-Wolfe, pp. 9, 13.

Every effort has been made to contact copyright holders of any material reproduced in this book. Any omissions will be rectified in subsequent printings if notice is given to the publisher.

Some words are shown in **bold**, like this.
You can find out what they mean by looking in the glossary.

Contents

What Is a Bank?

A bank is a business that offers services to its customers. All of these services have something to do with money. When someone puts money in a bank, the bank takes care of it. But, the person can use the money at any time.

People keep money in banks because banks are safe.

Banks differ in the services they provide and in how they are owned.

A bank can be big enough to fill a whole building. A bank can also be tucked into the corner of another business, such as a supermarket. No matter what the size, banks are the same in one way. They all offer services that help people use and save money.

A Safe Place for Money

Money in a pocket or purse can easily get lost or stolen. It is much safer to keep money in a bank. A bank puts money in a special room called a **vault.** A vault has strong locks and is fireproof.

No one can enter a bank vault without a bank guard.

The FDIC sign means that the government watches over the bank. FDIC means "Federal **Deposit** Insurance Corporation."

Banks also have security systems with locks and alarms. It is hard for anyone to steal money from a bank. The **government** helps keep money in a bank safe, too. There are many rules a bank must follow. These rules tell the bank what it can and can't do with the money people put there.

Bank Services

A bank takes care of money, but the money belongs to the person who put it there. It can be used whenever it is needed. A bank is a good place to save money for the future. The bank will keep the money safe.

Banks use the money people keep there to help other people and businesses.

Important papers and expensive jewelry are some of the items people put in safe-deposit boxes.

A bank is a place to borrow money, too. When people need money, a bank can help them. Banks also have safe-deposit boxes. People can keep important papers and valuable items in them. No one else can open the box.

Checking Accounts

A **checking account** is a bank service that lets people use money without having to carry **cash.** To open a checking account, a person gives some money to the bank. This is called making a **deposit.**

When using checks to pay for items, people must know exactly how much money they have in their checking accounts.

All the blank lines must be filled in with the correct information, and the account owner must write his or her name at the bottom.

The bank gives the person a **checkbook** with **checks** in it. A check is like a note telling the bank to pay some of the person's money to someone else. People can deposit money into their checking accounts whenever they want. They can also make **withdrawals,** or take money out of an account.

Savings Accounts

People open **savings accounts** to help them save for the future. Usually, money in a savings account is money they don't plan to use right away. People can **deposit** or **withdraw** money from their savings accounts whenever they want.

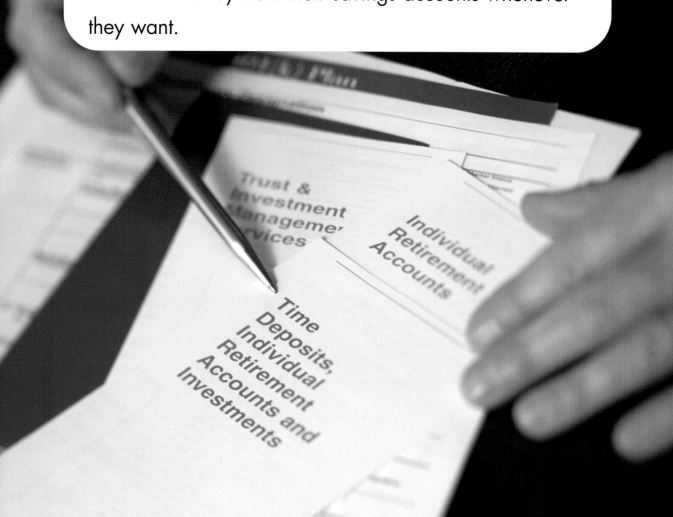

Most banks offer several different kinds of savings plans to help their customers save money for future use.

	Minimum	Interest Rate	Annual Percentage Yield
CURRENT RATES			
MONEY MARKET ACCOUNTS †			
VIP ACCOUNTS		02.85	02.89
PERSONAL BUSINESS	$50,000 $100,000	02.85	02.89
CUSTOM ACCOUNTS	$1,000 $2,000	02.25	02.27
PERSONAL BUSINESS	$10,000 $25,000	02.50	02.53
MONEY MARKET CERTIFICATES †			
31 Day	$500	02.25	02.28
91 Day	$500	02.50	02.53
182 Day	$500	02.60	02.63
1 Year	$500	02.85	02.89
INDIVIDUAL RETIREMENT ACCOUNTS †			
1 Year	$500	03.00	03.05
OTHER ACCOUNTS			
Regular Savings †	$100	02.25	02.28
	$10,000	02.50	02.53
Premium Checking †	$1,000	01.25	01.26
	$10,000	01.50	01.51
Combined Premium Account †		02.25	02.27

Please ask a New Account Representative for further information about applicable fees and terms.

There is a substantial penalty for early withdrawal, including substantial tax penalties on tax-deferred instruments.

† Simple interest
‡ Interest is compounded daily

Rates in effect thru: **Mar. 11th**
Member FDIC

THIS SYMBOL INSURES THE SAFETY OF YOUR FUNDS WITH US.

This sign tells how much interest the bank pays.

The bank uses the money in savings accounts to run its business. In return, the bank pays savings accounts customers a special **fee** called **interest.** The interest is added to the money in the account. The longer money stays in the account, the more interest it earns.

Loans

Most people don't have enough money to pay for expensive items like a house or car all at once. They can borrow part of what they need from a bank. The borrowed money is called a **loan.**

Most cars cost more money than people can spend at one time.

Banks make money by charging interest on loans.

Loans have to be paid back. The bank also charges **interest** on loans. The interest is added to the amount borrowed. People who get loans end up paying back more money than they borrowed. The bank charges more interest on a loan than it pays for **savings accounts.** This is one way a bank makes money.

Bank Cards

Banks offer special cards to their customers. **Credit cards** let people buy things now and pay for them later. Using credit cards is like getting a small **loan.** If the money isn't paid back right away, the bank charges **interest.**

The interest rate people must pay for using a credit card is much higher than for a small loan.

Debit cards look just like credit cards.

Debit cards work like **checks.** When people pay for things with debit cards, the money really comes from their **checking accounts.** Businesses must pay banks a **fee** every time someone pays them with a credit card or debit card. Banks make money from these fees and from the interest they charge on credit cards.

Working with Customers

Many people work in a bank. Some have jobs helping bank customers. A bank teller helps customers **withdraw** and **deposit** money in **checking** and **savings accounts.** Tellers work behind a counter. Customers walk up to the counter when they need to make a **transaction.**

This woman is giving her driver's license to the bank teller. The teller can then complete the transaction.

Loan officers try to get the best loans for their customers.

Bank officers help to open new accounts. They can also answer questions and give advice about money. **Loan** officers work with people who want to borrow money from the bank. They ask questions and help to fill out the papers needed to get the best loan for the customer.

Working Behind the Scenes

There are some bank workers who are never seen by customers. Accountants keep track of **deposits** and **withdrawals.** They pay the bank's bills and keep records about what it costs the bank to do business. Computer workers run the bank's computers. The computers add and subtract money from accounts. They figure out how much **interest** should be charged or paid to customers.

Accountants also make sure that the bank has enough money to stay in business.

Customer service representatives help customers who choose to do business by phone.

Customer service representatives do some of the same jobs bank tellers do. However, they do them over the phone. There are many other workers needed to run a bank. They might file papers, guard the bank doors, or decide how the bank uses the money in its **vault.** In some way, every worker's job is to offer service to the bank's customers.

Banking Without a Bank

Even when the bank is closed, people can use its services. They do this with special machines called **Automated Teller Machines,** or **ATMs.** An ATM can be used at any hour of the day or night.

Some ATMs are labeled with the name of a bank.

ATMs are usually located where many people go.

ATMs are hooked up to the bank's computers. That means they can do many of the things a bank teller does. ATMs are outside banks and in malls and supermarkets. There are even ATMs in little buildings all by themselves.

How an ATM Works

An **ATM** works with a special card. Sometimes the card is just for the ATM. But sometimes a **credit** or **debit card** can be used.

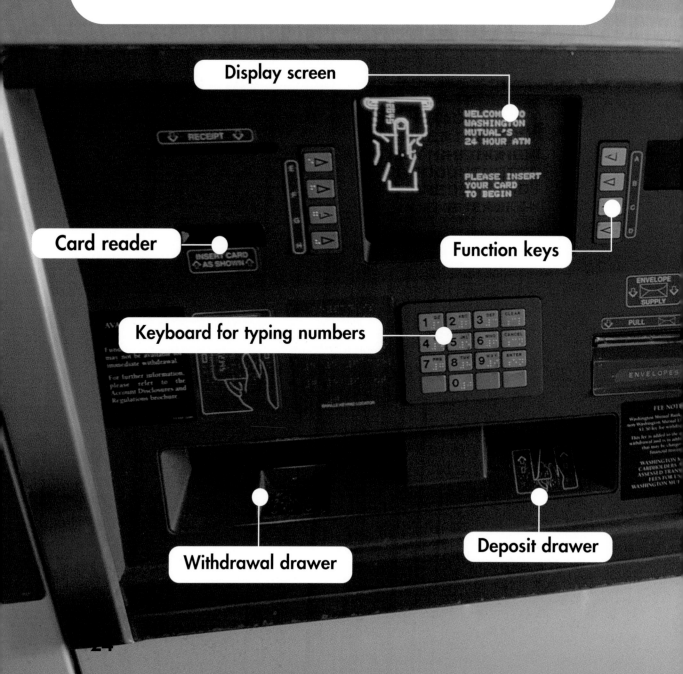

Display screen

Card reader

Function keys

Keyboard for typing numbers

Withdrawal drawer

Deposit drawer

The card has a code in a strip on the back. When the card is put into the ATM, the bank's computer reads the code. Then the ATM display screen asks the customer to type in a secret number called a personal identification number (PIN).

Next, the ATM asks the customer to push a **function key** to tell what he or she wants to do. The customer can make a **deposit** to or **withdrawal** from an account. Customers can even borrow money.

Keeping Track of Money

Banks keep careful records to show what happens to money. When someone **deposits** money, the amount is entered in the bank's computers. The computer prints out a **deposit slip** that tells how much money went into the account. If a customer makes a **withdrawal,** the computer prints out a **withdrawal slip.**

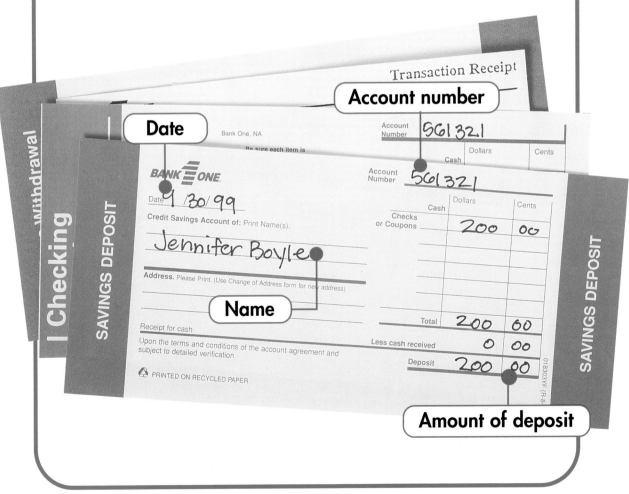

Date

Account number

Name

Amount of deposit

Transaction Receipt

Bank One, NA

Be sure each item is

BANK ☰ ONE.

Date 1/30/99

Credit Savings Account of: Print Name(s).

Jennifer Boyle

Address. Please Print. (Use Change of Address form for new address)

Receipt for cash

Upon the terms and conditions of the account agreement and subject to detailed verification

♻ PRINTED ON RECYCLED PAPER

	Account Number	561321	
		Dollars	Cents
Cash			

		Dollars	Cents
Account Number	561321		
Cash			
Checks or Coupons		200	00
Total		200	00
Less cash received		0	00
Deposit		200	00

SAVINGS DEPOSIT

I Checking

withdrawal

SAVINGS DEPOSIT

This withdrawal slip records the transaction that just took place.

Even if an **ATM** is used, the customer gets a deposit or withdrawal slip. The bank's computers keep track of every **transaction**. Once every month, customers get a **bank statement** in the mail. The statement describes everything that happened with the customer's accounts in that month.

Reading a Bank Statement

Customers need to read their **bank statements** carefully to make sure all their money is safe and that every **transaction** has been recorded. A bank statement like this one shows how many services banks offer.

A bank statement shows every transaction and what the bank does with the customer's money.

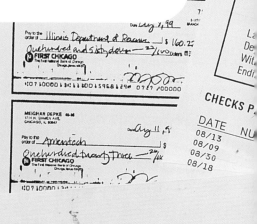

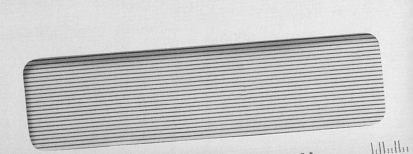

FIRST CHICAGO
The First National Bank of Chicago

Suite 0294
Chicago, Illinois 60670-0294

A *BANK ONE*. Company

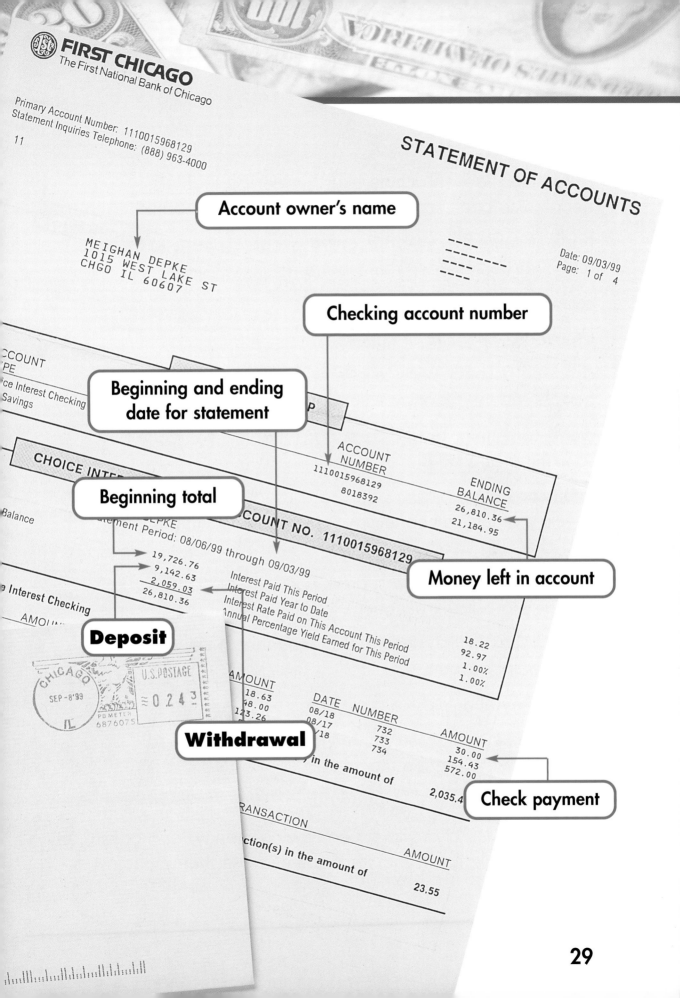

FIRST CHICAGO
The First National Bank of Chicago

Primary Account Number: 1110015968129
Statement Inquiries Telephone: (888) 963-4000

11

Account owner's name

MEIGHAN DEPKE
1015 WEST LAKE ST
CHGO IL 60607

Date: 09/03/99
Page: 1 of 4

Checking account number

Beginning and ending date for statement

ACCOUNT
NUMBER
1110015968129
8018392

ENDING
BALANCE
26,810.36
21,184.95

Beginning total

CHOICE INT

...ment Period: 08/06/99 through 09/03/99

Money left in account

19,726.76
9,142.63
2,059.03
26,810.36

Interest Paid This Period
Interest Paid Year to Date
Interest Rate Paid on This Account This Period
Annual Percentage Yield Earned for This Period

18.22
92.97
1.00%
1.00%

e Interest Checking

AMOU...

Deposit

CHICAGO
SEP -8'99
IL

U.S.POSTAGE
≈ 0 2 4 3
PB METER
6876075

AMOUNT
18.63
48.00
123.26

DATE NUMBER
08/18
08/17   732
/18   733
               734

AMOUNT
30.00
154.43
572.00

Withdrawal

in the amount of

2,035.4

Check payment

...RANSACTION

...ction(s) in the amount of

AMOUNT

23.55

Glossary

Automated Teller Machine (ATM) machine that lets people use bank services without going to the bank

bank statement written record of what happens to the money a person keeps in a bank

cash coins and paper money

checkbook booklet of checks

checking account service offered by a bank that lets people use their money without carrying cash

credit card thin, plastic bank card that lets someone buy something and pay for it later

debit card thin, plastic bank card used instead of a check, that lets someone pay for something with money in a checking account

deposit money put into a bank account; or, to put money into a bank account

deposit slip written record of money that is deposited into a bank account

fee money charged for a service

function key button on an ATM that lets customers choose how to use the machine

government leadership of a country, state, or town

interest money charged for borrowing money; or money paid to people for letting someone else use their money

loan money someone borrows

savings account service offered by a bank for saving money

transaction business deal done with a bank

vault room in a bank for keeping money and valuable objects

withdrawal money taken out of a checking or savings account

withdrawal slip written record of money that is taken out of a bank account

More Books to Read

Adelstein, Amy. *Money.* Vero Beach, Fla.: Rourke Publishers, 1997.

Armentrout, Patricia. *Protecting Money.* Vero Beach, Fla.: Rourke Publishers, 1996.

Sobczak, Joan. *Banking.* Vero Beach, Fla.: Rourke Publishers, 1997.

Index